TAP DANCING

FOR BIG MOM

ROSEANN LLOYD

TAP DANCING

FOR BIG MOM

ROSEANN LLOYD

Drawings by Arne Nyen

New Rivers Press 1985

Minnesota Voices Project Number 25

Typesetting: Peregrine Cold Type
Book Design: Gaylord Schanilec
Author Photo: Allen Simpson
The front cover painting, "Isabel, Voodoo
"Priestess," is by Arne Nyen

Acknowledgements: Some of these poems have appeared (sometimes in earlier ver-
sions) in the following publications: *Contact* , *Croton Review, Cutbank, Dark
Horse, Greenfield Review, Loonfeather, Milkweed Chronicle, Minnesota Monthly,
Sinister Wisdom*, and *Snowy Egret*. "Song of the Fisherman's Lover" appeared in
*Wetting Our Lines Together: An Anthology of Recent North American Fishing
Poems*; "Dreaming the Spring Garden," "Winter Solstice," and "Comfort"
appeared in *Where We Are Now: The Montana Poets Anthology*. "Tribe" first
appeared on a Mountains in Minnesota Collaborative Project broadside published
by *Milkweed Editions*; "Exorcism of Nice" first appeared on a broadside for the
Hungry Mind Bookstore Reading Series. Several of these poems were also broad-
cast over Minnesota Public Radio. The author wishes to thank the editors of
these publications for permission to reprint here. She also wishes to thank
Madeline, Dick, and Texx; Jan, Rich, Phebe, the Sunday Women Writers and,
especially, Brigitte, Nancy, Allen, and Deborah for the loving attention they have
given these poems.

Tap Dancing for Big Mom has been published with the aid of grants from the
following organizations: The Jerome Foundation, The First Bank System
Foundation, The Arts Development Fund of the United Arts Council, and The
McKnight Foundation.

New Rivers Press books are distributed by

Bookslinger	and	Small Press Distribution
213 East 4th St.		1784 Shattuck Ave.
St. Paul, MN		Berkeley, CA
55101		94709

Tap Dancing for Big Mom has been manufactured in the United States of
America for New Rivers Press, Inc. (C. W. Truesdale, editor/publisher), 1602
Selby Ave., St. Paul, MN 55104 in a first edition of 1,000 copies.

This book is dedicated to Karen Shaud
with love and gratitude.

1. BIO NOTES

2. EXORCISM OF NICE

3. LULLABYE FOR THE CHILD WITHIN

I
BIO NOTES

When I shoot off my mouth, I know I'm alive

But once I had set out,
I was already far on my way.

— Colette

TAP DANCING FOR BIG MOM

I'm sitting at the kitchen table, punching the color button of the oleo packet. It POPS like an egg but I can't feel the splatter in my fingers because the packet is thick as an innertube. I'm kneading the cold white dough inside until the orange marbles through it & it's not cold any more, now it's warm & the kitchen is sunny. Gramma is sitting next to me, pulling the feathers out of a chicken. The feathers are rusty in color. It's just me & her, sitting & talking. Nobody else is here. Of course there are other people in the house — there's Dora the Boarder who pours the water off the vegetables she cooks & saves it in the icebox in tall clear jars & drinks it later — Gramma says — for the vita-mins, but I never get to see her do it so I don't know for sure if she does. There's Marlene who rents the apartment upstairs where Aunt Tid used to live. Tid is short for her real name Matilda, the baby sister of my great-gramma, Minnie Tennessee. Marlene can throw her voice into her dummy who is bigger than her baby & is the one I will think of years later every time I see Candace Bergen in a movie & feel sorry for her because of her sibling rivalry with a wooden boy. Marlene combs her hair so it looks like it is painted on her head like the dummy's. During the War she travelled all over the Pacific Theater entertaining our boys. The Pacific Theater is a stage with waves painted on the backdrop in navy blue. That dummy is somewhere in this house now and so is my brother who is probably crawling around under the dining room table where we play train, pretending the metal handles that open the table's middle for leaves are actually the controls to the train engine we drive through the back hills to smuggle supplies for Robert E. Lee or Ulysses S. Grant — we can't ever make up our minds which one it is because nobody will tell us who won the War Between the States & we won't even know that there's another name for the War until we move to Minnesota & even then I won't understand the Southern confusion of names because Gramma's hero is Abraham first Who Freed the Slaves and Ike second Who Loves His Wife, the one he is smiling at on the china plate on the wall. Gramma is my hero & she's the one I want to be with now, here in the kitchen, & there's nobody here but us, sitting & talking. And even if my memory is kind of funny, it's just like Gramma's, for she will later deny that she ever had to buy oly — not during the War or at any other time. She always puts butter on her table. But right now she is asking me how do I like coloring the oly & do I want to hear her story about how her daddy made her go to school when she was 5 years old & she had to sit in the seat at the front of the row without a desk & her feet dangled & didn't touch the floor & now it's my turn to tell a story & I'm talking like a really good tap dancer, fast at first, and then real slow, with easy, unexpected turns, & she never says, stop being silly, she never says, stop exaggerating, she never says, stop talking in your Bible voice. She says, yes, & then what happened? What happens next? Nothing happens next. I never have to leave this border state, she never has to die, we're here in the kitchen surrounded by sun & chicken feathers & she's saying, go on, Rosie, go on.

BIO NOTES

I started writing   poems my teacher said
Too good for grade school what book
did you copy that from?
That was the year I squinted to see off
the blackboard   afraid to tell them
my eyes went bad   from reading
under the covers
just like my dad said

I started writing   in high school poems
were OK as long as you had some guy
on the string   Poems about loneliness   love
My family said *Be a teacher you'll always*
have a job   Look at our cousins
cousins by the wagonload   Off to Teachers College
Normal School   they used to call it
I wanted to be normal

I started writing   first teaching job   poems
Not telling the principal about
the professor who said   *These poems lack*
objective correlative and show emotional
instability not fitting a teacher   He was the one
who scanned the halls with his art-gum
erasing *FUCK* off the walls

I started writing busy poems   I was busy
working in the world   *Save the Planet*
Save the Ghetto   Stop the War
Art is a bourgeois luxury   a personal solution
not part of THE Solution   you know what I mean
this is a busy stanza   I didn't think about
how I was jealous of my friend in high school
playing the concert stage in Bavaria and that other boy
off to the Butterfield Blues Band

I started writing   at home with a baby   poems
writing in despair   the knot of family secrets
my brother's death notebooks   writing
broken marriage   poems   broke   on my own   out
of work   lacking in objective correlative   resorting
to personal solutions   unable to save   brothers
sisters   coherence   anybody's   marriage   ghetto

I started writing poems   driving down
the valley to the Old Poet himself who said
You like the other girls — divorced?   huh?   suicidal?
I said   *It's easy to give the poems*
up for all the good & foolish   reasons   But I started
writing poems   this time   old enough
in my fits and starts   to know
I need to keep what keeps coming back
what keeps starting again

LOVE POEM FOR MIDDLE AGE

Look, Old Beak, spring
is here! The puddle ducks
are tunneling
their necks through the mud
for food. Pollen green
shoes! The runners
scoot along, their rock-n-roll
transistors squawk
and the IDS Tower — looking
rangy — flashes
sundown, its fiery
lavenders not quite
making it I'm referring
to the intensity of the Sapphire
Mountains I said I'd never
leave.   I said I'd

never come back
to High School City, Health
City, where everyone
strides for the picture
of perfect health. They say
there are houses here
over whose threshold   garlic
has never passed. Pleasant
ghettos — they say — Black,
Red, Indifferent, Those
of the Norwegian
Persuasion, where a woman
could die of the three-piece

bland. But the 60's dropped
me here again, middle-aged
and crotchety just like
everybody else. I'm getting
thick around the middle,
our children bite their
fingernails. Look, Old Beak,

look over there!

There's a kid perched
halfway up that pine tree —
she's throwing sticks
down at her little brothers,
taunting

What next? What next?

TV HEARTH

Sick in bed
after surgery on my eye
my mind worried   every
noise   *What is that scrape
on metal? Chicken soup
for lunch?   Why   can't I
get better faster   what if
these ears have to
become my eyes?*

I got the tv
in bed with me so its
steady drone and whine
could short out
the mind's incessant
whys   It did cut off
reality but still
its flicker blueing
white batted at my eyes

*flicker   flicker   rest
flicker   flicker   rest*

The eyes were made to pay
attention   watch a cat
catnapping   keeping
track   what moves when
and where   *What's that
fuzz scooting under
the chair?*

Where the eyes go   the mind
follows and   draws its muscles
to alert   attention
muttering   *The blind
leading the carcass*

worry   worry   rest
worry   worry   rest

What the eyes need
to knock   it off   this
constant functioning
is a nice gray cave
that doesn't move that
talks   a telethon on
channel 2   when the tv
stops its twitchy
flickers   hitches up
for one wide shot
The screen is big
and bland and still

The eyes stay shut
and the ears keep
track . . . *the long and short*
of it is   to pledge
call 227-1122 and your
thoughts recite
the catechism of healing:

WHAT IS THE HIGHEST PURPOSE
OF THE EYES ON EARTH?

The purpose and glory of the eyes
is tracking the leaf
a cat or other beast
that lurks at the door of the cave.

WHAT IS THE SOLEMN DUTY
OF THE EARS ON EARTH?

The solemn duty of the ears
is singing the eyes
to sleep

WHAT, THEN,
OF OUR NEWEST SENSE — TV?

The tv turns the singing body

down to monotone, singing, sung

slowed down
as a lizard nodding

rest   rest   rest

on a flat gray rock

utterly thoughtless

utterly blasé

GREYHOUND STANDARD TIME

Anna fidgets the last leg of this trip, insists
it's time to read. I keep losing
my place, visions of DeNiro sprawled
on a bed. *Charlotte sat moodily*
eating a horsefly . . . A man slips close
by us to listen, his baby blue T-shirt glitters
CALIFORNIA. Across the aisle,
a child-mother feeds her baby
French fries. *It was a delicious meal —*
rind of a summer squash, stale toast, scum
off a cup of cocoa. California-glitter leans
over to see Wilbur, the radiant pig. Closed-in
smoke and sweat, more persistent in the dark.
Not enough mothers to go around.
                                        I feel fat and
tired. Jeans ripping, coffee slopped down
my coat. Pretensions to elegance,
continual entropy. Our sleeping bag slides
to the floor, scummy, and my voice goes
harsh, *Anna, get up & sit still.*
Do you want me to read or not? I admit it,
I'm a bitch. I've spent my life in Russian
novels, wanting the nerves
of a peasant. This raising of children, it
makes a serious assault on the ego. Sara
Dylan — arrested for assault on her children's
teacher. The bus lurches off
the freeway, swerves to another small town
where nobody gets on. All the missing fathers.
It's hard to stick it out.
                              They don't catch
anything, said Charlotte. They just keep trotting
back and forth. The bald man
in front of us throws an arm back over the seat.
That lazy motion breaks my bad mood. A baby

who can't walk yet crawls all over its mother.
Sometimes I feel that thumping
stronger than anything, her brand-new breath
fresh as baking soda. Suddenly it seems
the only real suspense in life
is waiting for a baby and this sloppy air sprawls
delicious as any lover's bed, the bus sways
and trots toward the smoggy horizon
of the over-grown cow-town. I pull Anna gently
up into my lap, pick up the book and begin
again. *Does anybody here know how
to spell the word TERRIFIC? Charlotte
asked petulantly.*

My friends who don't have children

sit uneasy in my house   cross
their legs   say   look   the soy sauce
crystallized down the stove
at loss   things continue
to move   the newspapers
pile on the floor   pajamas
on the table   the dust doesn't sit
reliably in place   my friends
don't want to be jostled
out of place   they say
I like kids really and take off
after whatever it is
they're after   the poem
singing its perfect
music   Chicken Kiev seasoned
to perfection   the Big O or XKE
right in time   *everything*   I say
in my own good time   it's not
that I dislike my friends   their
houses are a slow motion refuge
where you can predict the quality
of light   the position
of the chairs and even the cat
manages to keep its tail
I can sit still there   it is
still there   spoons
don't drop to the floor   as I said
it's not that I dislike
my friends   it's just
that I don't like to think
why they can't sit with me
in the house I need to get home to
nights: that raspy breathing
in the adjacent room

POOR HIM

What a wonderful bird the frog are
When he sit he stand almost
When he hop he fly almost
He ain't got no sense hardly
He ain't got no tail hardly either
When he sits he sits on what he ain't got almost.
— Anonymous

Poor Him wants more and more
Poor Him ain't got enough
of what him gots hardly
Him wants happy house   kids over
make pies   party   party   laughs
a minute   Him say   *Gimme*
more than too-much-kids
They dress up real nice
Go Gutree   Poor Him say   *More*
movies   They go movies   Him say
Why you never go stores?
They go shop shop   Poor Him
say   *How come you buy this bed?*
Don't got no more money   Poor
Him   Poor   Him!

Her say   *What you want most*
Poor Him?   Him say   *Me want*
spontaneity   go café
eat cheap   cheese   more
wine   They go galleries for free
Poor Him say *Gimme more cheap*
sex in daytime   They do it
today   Poor Him say   *Too-much-*
stuck-at-home   Her take him
walk lake   Poor Him goes
Boring Nature Poet Shit!
Gimme more   Gimme   parties   pies
kids   laughs a minute   shop
shop   more money   more cheap
sex!   Poor Him! Poor Him!

25

Poor Him work hard   do more above
and beyond   hardly never complain
Never say   MAD   SAD   GLAD
hoard it all up   Poor Him
don't cry   No way José
Him not whine neither   Don't confide
nobody where it hurt   it don't hurt
cuz her hop to it
fix it up   *Hurry   Hurry*   Hoppin'
frog-busy — not this   not that —
for the Boss of Say-So as in
I gots the Say-So
less and more, how much, not enough?

Poor Him gets more and more
Her gets lots o' less
Her hop so much-not-enough
Her shrink tiny   Her frog-tail
gettin' to be was-tail
waggin' and stumpin' along
slidin'   down
that old hole of less-'an-herself
til what's more are nothin'-left
Poor Him sit on what he ain't got hardly
Him gots vim and vigor
Him hang on life and limb
Too late   Poor Him!   Poor Him!

Poor Him peek over the gone
No Her   where Her used to be
Did Her hop 'til her fly
or sink 'til her SWIM?
Poor Him mutter
Her not gone enough hardly
Me take cuisinart   Go check out
pollywogs   They gimme
They gimme more!   Poor Him
talk it up   talk marathon
mutter   mutter   rattle on
Poor Him do carry on
ain't got no sense hardly
sittin' there talkin'   *GIMME   GIMME*
in that bright shinin' light
all   gone

(last two lines repeat)

THE OTHER SIDE OF ANGER IS NOT FEAR

What happens to the dreams of young mothers?
— Adrienne Rich

1
I tend her like a sleepwalker.
In her sickness we regress
to that first intense gazing
she can't remember. I rock her,
touch her face, say lightly
eyes, nose, chin-chopper, chin.
It doesn't work. My breath waits
for hers. I measure the nights
with glasses rimmed with burgundy,
damp gowns flung down on the floor.
I rock and watch the ceiling.
There's a stain fat as a map of India
dark as wine spilled on the sheets.
It shifts like steam, like codeine
in the bowl of a spoon, careless
as the flush on her cheeks.

2
Someone is cutting her fingernails.
Now they're cutting her fingers,
throwing them away. Daddy is losing again,
white fingers are dice, green
neon in Vegas, dark roses thrown down on
Philip's snowy grave. Faces
swaddled in bandages, the children eat
all the pills in the house:
aspirin is popcorn, butter is lye.
I pick up the fingernails,
pale slivers of moon, and paste
and paste blue eyes.

3

That shape shimmers
like hands in front of my face. Tell me
it's sun-up, a sudden rain. Don't
talk about sacrifice, the pleasures
of a life apart. This is my life.
I do what I have to do.
Rest the night. If I can only sleep,
tomorrow I will be O.K. I need
your arm thrown across my shoulder,
the lazy breath of sleep that's shared.
Hold me. Touch my face.
From our common breath, my lullabye.

WORDS BEFORE THEY GATHER

Sometimes making love
it settles in my left thigh
that place the stairs hit
the time the drunk landlord left the trapdoor up
and the lights off. My brother
fell down that cellar once, too, but that fall
wasn't what killed him. As for the landlord,
he is not dead, he's outliving his sister Marie
who bailed him out thirty years
and went real fast. There's no accounting for it.

Cigarette butts in the tub, I yell
at my brother, *Who do you think you are?*
It comes on, his voice,
You've got a raunchy mouth, woman,
as if we're taking arguments
to old age together, until I remember
him dead at twenty, not even half
a life. Our father moaned, *This death
is selfish.* I hear my voice answering,
Only the dead can know. Left behind
at the funeral, we can't know, we try, how
to manage living. How helpless all of us
were that day: the friend who stood by me
wearing her dead mother's coat of unborn lamb —
my mother, the child just buried
the one she loves best of all — the lover
who spooned chilled yogurt in my mouth, afraid
to father children — the man who was my husband
accusing, *The trouble
with you is your family,
drunk, divorced or dead.*

There's no accounting for it, though
there's reason enough. This anger
at the havoc they leave behind.
But, again, the dead, selfish? Only they
can know. One thing we can know
that's good and selfish
is making love
even when it brings them back — sprawled
there, half-conscious
on the moist and graying sheets.

These voices
for the graves of the living.
When I shoot off my mouth, I know I'm alive.

COMFORT

My hands cuddle the fruit in the bath, wipe the dirt off easy,
lift the slick bodies to the towel. My daughter, newborn, her
bottom, the small cleft and curve.

I don't sleepwalk any more, hugging her whimpers and panic.
And you, repeating love is physical, you write of desert photographs
and death, your fear of returning.

My hands know a hundred ways to bathe and cool you. Peaches,
gold in the cellar. You, bringing coffee to bed. Your hands. Calm
that means more than the common sense you call it.

What I forgot is I'm tired. This work gives steady order to
my day, to my thoughts, connection. I need your letters, pictures
of juniper, and all that I can't ask.

SOUTHEAST ASIA, SECOND GRADE

When the art class washes black
over their secret crayola drawings
Blong's Spiderman
pulls a green net across
the watery page. When we write
poems that begin *I Remember*
Blong designs
a Mercedes limousine, the military
detail, exact. In dream
poems, he colors a ship
with two anchors
a ship whose stars and stripes
shine turquoise, orange, and green.
He prints slowly
I'm the one who eats ghosts.
He's the one who searches
all the books for more
designs: a pink brontosaurus grins
and hops, his Arapaho
eagle rises like fire, Norwegian
serpents curl
to bronze, aquamarine and Spiderman
comes back again
and again without a sound
to my desk, to my lap —
the scraps, Manila, white
paper in sixteen folds.
And I'm the one
with the wide Caucasian face
who stares inscrutably
at the nets that bind. Down the hall
the soldiers' boys, pencils in fists,
grudge out the calligraphy of punishment —
I WILL NOT EXPLODE IN CLASS —
these sentences
knotting inside
one hundred times.

HUNTING FOR GROUSE

It's the yellow time when tamarack sheds.
The evening feeding time, when
trees and rain cut the light
to shreds. There's a woman walking through it.
Past the woman along the creek, a man
walks hidden from her view.

The woman walks and thinks of birds,
how they covey in the brush, flush and fly
before the gun comes up, sometimes whirring
from behind. The woman walks thinking
of birds, not thinking of them. The rain
closing in the woods, the tang of rot

pungent in the rain, who is the man
calling her? Is it the one who fashioned
rabbit gloves, the one who favors lace —
or one she doesn't know at all? What if she
pulls him down to leaves and feathers? This
continual calling over the other hill.

Walking stops the voices. The ease
of walking, her hips, the slip
boots make on deadfall in the rain.
Her eyes scan the ground for Kinnikinic,
the split red berries trail the birds to cover.
Twilight brush, mottled gray and brown.

That light on Sundays through yellowed lace.
It was Gramma who did the killing. Her
freckled hands twisted the Banty's neck,
dressed it, trussed it. She took the heart
for gravy. Those tiny bones crackled
under her hands, like underbrush . . .

The bird flies up. The woman stops,
is thinking how a bird's heart is suspended —
a womb between a woman's hips.
She shoots for the head. Waits
'til the eyes cloud over, then
kneels to strip the feathers

to muscle cupped smooth as the upper arm.
He calls to her now, the man who's walking.
His shadow wanders across the filtering
light. The woman looks up —
remembers the one walking with her.
When he steps out to meet her,

she touches the tamarack in his beard.

NOSTALGIA MINUS MEMORY

these new men with short hair
not-curls-around-the-collar hair
I'm talkin' about short *short* hair
greased-down-flat hair
high-fashion-nostalgia hair

these new men with short hair

they've got no memory
no history
when they sleep
they do not dream

of the old men with short hair
that-boy-cleans-up-real-nice hair
you-know-what-I'm-talkin'-about-now hair

the men with short hair
the ones who schemed to stash chemicals
in Castro's shoes
their women in dresses
stitched too tight to walk in
turned on
the wiretaps in the bedroom
of Martin Luther King
trip trap trip trap went the high heels

these new men with short hair
stuck-up-with-gel-hair
hair-the-way-it-used-to-be hair

these men with short hair

they've got no history
when they sleep
they do not dream

of the old men with short hair
cold-ear hair
violate-the-flesh hair

the ones who hauled the pigs
to the A-BOMB site
their uniforms were real clean
drove around in station wagons
got their wives pregnant
after the war   in peace
beat em up   beat em up

these new men with short hair
cold-ear hair
high-fashion-nostalgia hair

these new men with short hair

they've got no memory
when they sleep
they do not dream

of the old men with short hair
violate-the-flesh hair
you-know-what-I'm talkin'-about-now hair

the ones who beat up the fags & beatniks
messed with their daughters
whipped their sons with their belts
cheerful every morning
singing *rise & shine   rise & shine*

these are the men with short hair
I'm talkin' about short *short* hair
violate-the-flesh hair

they got me by the short hairs
toss & turn in my sleep
gimme whiskey   whisker burn   Dutch rub
rub my sleep the wrong way
rise   &   shine in my dreams
singing *beat em up   beat em up*
trip trap trip trap click the high heels

these men with short hair

violate-the-flesh hair
hair-the-way-it-used-to-be hair
that-boy-cleans-up-real-nice-hair

they've got   no memory

no history

they do not dream
when they sleep

they do not dream

when they sleep

II
EXORCISM OF NICE

Deaf and Dumb/Stupefied/Shut-down/Stunned

*Jesus said, "If you bring
forth what is within you, what
you bring forth will save you.
If you do not bring forth
what is within you, what you
do not bring forth will destroy
you."*

— *The Gnostic Gospels,*
Edited by Elaine Pagels

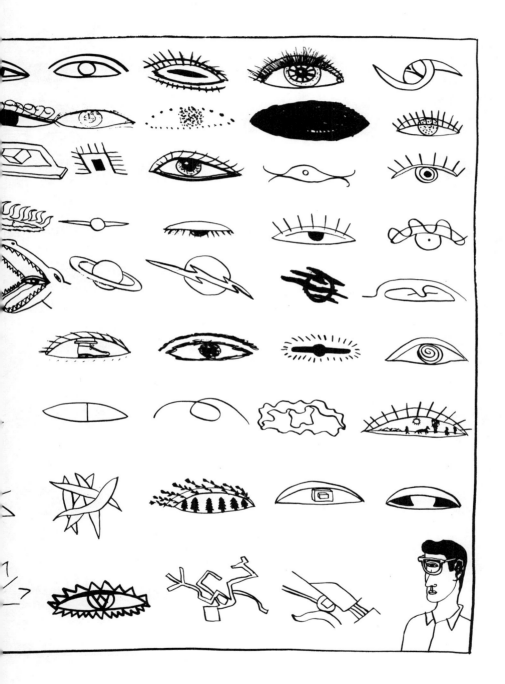

WINTER SOLSTICE

It always snows on your birthday,
drifting thick on the roof, the trees,
and every year I walk towards
that room on the second story.
I sleep in an upstairs room and walk
through other houses, other rooms.

Your last birthday, frost on the window
brittle and chipped,
a man on *The New Yorker*
watches the falling snow.
He's turned away
from his brushes and paint
and the cat at his feet
curled like the one you painted, that
cheshire we hid in the closet.
The night nobody could reach you
the snow was falling thick and light.
Feathers know this deception
of air, why the snow
may cover the earth, why
you smothered in a rush of flight.

It always snows on your birthday.
There's always the man at the window
watching the days that turn me
from you. Always the snow.
I sleep in an upstairs room. I wait
for the man to turn,
paint what he has seen. Thick, white
smears, strokes of feathery black.

Philip Leslie Skelton
December 20, 1951 — December 20, 1971

THE NEW HOUSE, WELCOMING

I feed it nothing but *dolce cantatas.*
On my knees, I mulch the beds around it.
The soft summer leavings
must muffle the wind from the mountain ash.

Walking gently by every window well
I promise my favorite childhood tales.
I bring bribes of apples, stir the fragrance
all day, the sweet autumn sauce.

It won't shut up. Contrary, the stairs
shift in fits and starts. The furnace
fidgets and taunts. Curtainless,
the windows yawn at my efforts.

Supper commotion, Mother is still
whistling in the kitchen.
I know her eyes
are cast down, her eyelashes whisper.

Now she's upstairs brushing her teeth.
Those years of covers moving smoothly,
her sighs more quiet
than breathing. Some nights

I get up at 3 to kick radiators.
Daddy burps the Smucker's lid, sticky
butterscotch. His noises down there,
the basement late show, slosh

like a broken washer 'til dawn. My daughter
kicks the covers, calls out her little
Appaloosa horse. Sloughing the door,
shoes, mail, her father comes in.

That unpredictable rummage. What he
must have to himself. We settle
the house, uneasy. Mother's soft
voice sounds as if through a house

sectioned to apartments, archways
papered over. The murmur of words
I can't make out. Her loneliness
and mine. I say, *Hush, house,*

let me sleep out this difference.

INSECT IS AN ANAGRAM FOR INCEST

1
hands spider their way
     under the covers   silky
secretions spin out
       webs in all the bright
         and shadowed corners.

     hands quiet as silverfish
burrow the night and day
       startle the leather-bound books
        sleeping in the attic

      glassy eyes twitch after footfalls
   especially those that amble
      towards the wicker couch
     flowering in the basement
      hunch-back beetles
       peer out
        the fruit cellar
        the motionless blue jars

2
No room in the house is safe.
Not any nook or cranny.
Not the dusty closet under the eaves
cozy as summer woods.
Not the cave under the bed
surrounded
by the spread's soft tassles.
Not the cushioned window seat
on the second-story
landing. Not the bay window
with its paisley satin pillows
and one thousand peacock
eyes opening
to the neighboring fields.

There are skitters everywhere
and footsteps, fingers, breath across
the back of the neck.

The burrows under the snowball bushes
that lead to the cool dark
under the large and rambling porch
look lovely as Grandmother's lap.

Skitters, whispers, harsh
breath across
the back
of the neck.

3
What can be done to rid the house of fear?
Scrub down the floors
Burn the curtains and drapes
Fumigate
Air the books on the sunny grass lawn
Sweep the ceilings with the rag-covered broom
Mothballs in the cupboards and eaves
FRESH PAINT FRESH
PAIN surely white
enamel allows nothing to hide

cobwebs spin out
from the glistening corners   Eggs bubble
up from under the surface
sheen and the anagram tiles
face down
in their drawer spell out
the insect names over and over

4

Even though the bathroom tiles
have been scrubbed with Lysol
Even though the dishes are stacked in order
Even though the beds
are stripped and changed and the toys
sorted and put away

The Tinker Toys   standing at attention
in their cardboard tower
twist and flap their hands

The bride doll locked in her train case
with the net and sequined trousseau
scratches at her face

The diamond blocks
arranged in their patterned box
perfect as the perfect pattern on the lid
grind chips of paint
off their wooden sides

And in the box that pictures maple trees and cloudless sky
the tiny men in red shirts
crackle their guns
like matchsticks struck
by curious children

In the drawer of the dining room buffet
the anagram tiles
click out
the secret letters once again

5
My father's fingers skip spider feet
across my skin   my mother
was eaten alive   the paper on my desk crumbles
under the nub of the pen   and the child
in my home   hunches over   she
starts at every approach   outside
my window   the wet sheets
rise up from the line   billow
wild — monster crawdads
springing on the wind

MEMO FROM MR. LEESON

When I happened upon the three-hole
Hummer Punch you sent us
for repair, I carefully took it apart
in an effort to locate its malfunction.
It appears this punch was over-
loaded, that is to say, too much
paper at one time. The condition
of the shaft where it contacts
the punch pins
and the punch pins themselves   lead
me to believe this.
Of course, a defective shaft
or defective pins   or both
could have caused the problem.

But whether the punch was over-loaded
or not is of no concern to me now.
I am sending another Hummer Punch.
If you should have a future
quality problem, do not hesitate
to write or call. In any case, please
remind those who use the punch
to watch
how much paper
they punch at one time.
I cannot tell you
how much   that is. But you can do
as I do. Do the best you can
with what you've got. I cannot
tell you   how much
that is.

PARAMETERS: ONE WOMAN'S DICTIONARY

1 If a man calls you *Angel*,
 he's afraid to die

2 If a man calls you *Darlin'*,
 he longs to be the outlaw
 of his own tragic life

3 If a man calls you *Companion*,
 he'll keep you
 from knowing your own way

4 If a man calls you *Generous*,
 he'll say *Be good to yourself*
 when he goes back to his wife

5 If a man fears death
 he may want to speak your name

6 If a man calls you *Lady*,
 he'll dress you in lace and kiss
 off the honest bitch

7 If a man calls you *Bitch*,
 he wants your tongue, wants
 a *Madonna, Dollie, Honey-Pie*

8 If a man eats you up, adores
 the *Gypsy, Waspwaist, Whore*,
 he won't make the bed

9 If a man doesn't fear death
 he won't know why he calls you
 Baby, slaps your face

10   If a man calls his mother
     Nag, give him
     time. He'll do the same for you

11   If a man calls you *Girl*, he will
     forever

12   If a man knows all these names
     and is silent, let him choose his own:
     Manchild, Kid Brother, Lover, Prince
     of Darkness, Mother-bear,
     Old Man on the Couch,
     Receiver-of-dreams,
     The-One-Who-Gives-Them-Back,
     Friend.

EXORCISM OF NICE

Mum's the word
Taciturn
Talk polite
Appropriate
Real nice
Talk polite
Short and sweet
Keep it down
Quiet down
Keep the lid on
Hold it down
Shut down
Shut up
Chin up
Bottle up
Drink up
Up tight
Tied up in knots
Tight-lipped
Hold tight
Tongue-tied
Hold your tongue
Hold still
Hold it back
Hold it in
Hold your cards close to your chest
Close-mouthed
Muzzled
Gagged
Garbled
Jammed up
All wrapped up
Tied up
Shut up
Zonked out
Tucked in
Caved in

Shut in
Locked in
Incoherent
Inarticulate
In a shell
Shell-shocked
Thunder-struck
Dumb-struck
Deaf and Dumb
Stupefied
Shut-down
Stunned

Oh, Wicked Mother of the Kingdom of Silence
I have obeyed you
long enough.

OH

W.C. Fields, that fat old mother of Speak Your Mind, outrageous
even on death's bed:
> *When I think of all my money, I think of all the little orphans*
> *who could use some change, then, on the other hand, I say Fuck 'em*

It is reported that when women lay dying
90% murmur *OH*

When women lay beaten
it is said   they cover their faces
and murmur   *OH*

Opaque   cream   smooths
a new skin
        of the face
               Trusty blue
mascara   fastens eyes
to innocence
        The arch
to the brows
        alerts intelligence
And the sweet
        bright red
           holds
the mouth
        perpetually open
            in its
perpetual

OH

This mask is strong and real
like life
but more reliable. It will not tic
or flutter. It will not show
fear nor any other
motion
        except for the mouth
             offering
                  its cheery *OH*

    And the name of the mask is *Smile-pretty-now-never-mind*
    The name of the mask is *Suffer-in-silence, Carry-on*
    The name of the smile is *Lookin' good*
    The name of the mouth is *Sorrow.*

OH she said when he sucker-punched
her in the bar *OH* she said again
on the heating pad in bed *OH*
she breathes into the world
Thin puffs of disbelief

never enough air for one clear sound
for YES for NO for
LET ME THINK THAT OVER

  OH   the half-sigh breath-that's-not-enough
     giving in
         even as it goes

    The name of this breath is *Scared-to-death*
    The name of this death is *Suffer-in-silence China Doll*
    The name of the doll is *Little Mother of Disbelief*
    The name of the doll is *Lost*
    The name of her smile is *Sorrow.*

If you break a doll, it does not cry out
Help me.

If you take a doll to W.C. Fields movies
it mutters *bad-mouth trash.*

If you wind a doll up
it sings:
> *Victim once*
> *Victim twice*
> *I'd rather be beaten*
> *Than scared all my life*

> And the name of this song is *Raggedy Wife*
> The name of her dress is *Catch-my-breath*
> The name of her breath is *Dragged-out-death*
> The name of her death is *Porcelain Doll*
> The name of her smile is *Sorrow.*

When it expires, that last
devoted OH,
it won't hurt at all, the practiced
half-breath
giving in
even as it goes.

> But the name of Mother is *Lots-more-left*
> The name of Mother is *Curse-your-death*
> The name of Mother is *Spit-it-out*

The Fat Old Mother called *Love-yourself-enough*
> will give you
> > breath enough
> to say what you need to say.

Beginning with OH

Say with full   slow breath
Say *Mother I'm scared he hit me*
    Mother he touched me   funny
        Mother   don't turn your face away

For the name of Mother is *More-than-enough breath*
The name of Mother is *Lots-more-left*

Her breath will carry you   beyond your sorrow
beyond your death

Your breath will give *Sorrow* a brand-new name:

    Sorrow, your name was *Dog-at-my-throat*

    Sorrow, your name was *Smile-pretty-now-never-mind*

    Oh, Sorrow,
                we will name you   *Left-behind.*

    Oh, *Sorrow,*
                when we finally name you

                we finally let you
                        let us go

HOW THE MIND RELEASES
WHAT MEMORY REFUSES TO KNOW —
THE LUNCHROOM,
SUNSHINE SCHOOL, SIXTH GRADE

What one does with incest is to compress it,
to make it tiny, make it small; to fit it
into the smallest space possible, after
eliminating the details . . . Whatever detail
there is, is part accident, part defiance.

                          — Anne Lee

Browsing in a used bookstore
I come across a picture of Marilyn Monroe
her breasts
spilling out of a red dress
on the cover of L I F E magazine
and it brings back the era
when my dad comes in and lays on me
whispering

Don't you want me
to rub them
so they'll get big and beautiful
like Marilyn Monroe   full of milk
full of life
your husband will love them
it says in the Bible
don't be a homo

and the only way
to slip free of his grip is to
slip into the picture
which his words are making in my mind —

the bright red carton
sturdy as a barn
waxy as lipstick
red as the dress Marilyn tipped out of
on the cover of L I F E magazine
the tall white letters
spilling
H O M O   W H O L E   M I L K

out onto the shiny black surface
of the hot lunch tray

THIS CHILD

this child is about to be touched
touched funny   told to shut up

about the fast lesson down   how
if you rub a nipple   it sticks out

hard   this child is about to hide
her nipples inside her shirt   inside

her undershirt   this child is about
to be forced to do without

a father   hurts too much
this child is about to cry at his touch

about to run and hide
this child is about to be deprived

of childhood   it's all shut up
this child is about to be touched

by the power of a man who lies
who will disregard her cries

call her *seductive/beautiful/slut*
this child is about to give up

clothes silky to the touch   hide
her nipples inside her shirt   this child

will give her childhood up
her own tentative touch

her imagination playing free and wild
the daydreams of a child   this child

will be gone at his touch
offered up   shut up

REMEMBERING IN THREE PARTS

1
When I remember I have no father
I want to cut off my hands. If I do
not have any hands, I do not have anything
to wring like a girl. If I am not
a girl, I cannot grow up
to be a woman. If I am
not a woman, I have no feelings
in my womanly parts and cannot touch
them with my hands. Neither can I
touch any other creature
with affection.

2
When I remember I have no father
I remember the nights I stayed up reading
to block out the pain and the psychologist
in the room next door pacing
his *sleep deficit*, hour after hour
of accumulating lack.
He said he'd never catch up. Even
in the winter the stand-up fan
beat itself across the floor. Once he
showed me how he shaved
his teddy bear. I tried to cover
my revulsion, said I had no problem
with mutilation. No problem with childhood
love, the deprivation thereof.

In this troubled extremity, my wrists
tingle. I say I must unhand
myself, curse the lack, walk
away. But the feet below
stumble on trouble, are troubled, can't
remember *left-right*
without their fellow hands.

3

When I remember I have no father, I need
a laying on of hands, hands
that do not mind my phantom
pain, hands that touch
the centering parts, remembering me:
third-eye, nose, mouth, breast-
plate, belly
button, shining button.
Folded in
to this connection, mind, mine, I can unfold
and feel the length
of my extremities, the paradox of dualities,
how a body moves by twos —
arms, legs, centered-stretched,
loved-bereft, breasts,
my hands.

My hands, remembered now, remember
that they belong to me. They begin again
with useful work and love —
making patches, cooking stew, putting
things away. But they never
discover the place to hold
the words for *father:*
lack, deficit, deprivation of.

PRAYER FOR HEALING

Our Mother who is this earth
Your name is always holy.
Your nation has already arrived, here, in the body.
May we sense what the whole cosmos is and is becoming
Both in the body and in the spirit.
May we make our own bread every day.
And may we transform our anger, hatred, and despair.
Do not lead us into self-loathing.
Save us from our longing to damage ourselves.
For ecstasy is yours — mind, body, and breath —
Forever and ever.

DREAMING THE SPRING GARDEN

Don't mull it over with your fingers. Don't ask whether you're here because you took Mother's advice on how to carry scissors, *closed, points down, don't run*. Don't brood about whether sardines are hermetically sealed. It doesn't hurt to give up clocks. Give up cutting and pasting articles. *George Seversen Crawls 1,000 Miles for Jesus.* Shoe polish and suicide require too much concentration. Have confidence in yourself. Pick lint. I know you can find the bathroom. Think of Howard Hughes urinating into Mason jars. Nobody cares if you eat out of tin cans. Sit on the couch, watch it snow, think about mending your head with vinegar and brown paper. Read Peter Rabbit.

I know your hands remember summer folded up on itself like a steel vegetable steamer. Panic is a bad smell from old kitchens. Think of cabbage moths feasting on finger leaves.

It is of little consequence that your fingers play Debussy in the flesh of your lover's back. Indulge the thick taste in your mouth with sauerkraut. Ignore old friends. Read Peter Rabbit. Imagine black-eyed peas, bloating and sprouting in loam, unfolding like cabbages. Dream of your French braids, Grandma's narrow walk. Dream forsythia, thickets with burrows. The tar baby. Soft-boiled eggs and milk like cream on the ferry to Denmark.

Though your hands shake, you're dreaming steadily the woman walking toward you. The one in the sunhat, tending the spring garden and laughing.

IF IT'S NIGHT

Home is where you count on things: belts, hammers, brooms. . . . The backs of books are never broken. If it's night, you can stay up late reading. Nobody's going to crawl under the covers.

Four-year-old legs open like a well-thumbed paperback. Memory flutters shut in a rustle of shadows. *Mother Goose* and *The Book of Giants*, scribbled with green crayola. Why does she whimper? The older girl hugs her breasts against the sheet. She can't forget. It wasn't cold.

No funeral for father in that bed. Dream cradle. Skirts of milky petals. Creatures with fluted wings. Believe me, you won't be bedridden for life. Soon, you will carry boxes of Nancy Drew to the good-will store and begin to plot the story of innocence which you give to yourself. The story nobody can read till you let him. When he says there's something childlike about your face, you'll rock him, whisper *welcome home*.

VISIONS OF THE SOLSTICE

The children are sleeping
and *visions of sugar plums*, we say,

dance through their heads

even though we know
it is the children themselves

who are the plums
and the visions of the plums

which the mother-and-father
watch over, guard
                    — *the AND we are living for* —
and cherish
for it is not yet their time —;

THE CHILDREN ARE SLEEPING

it is not yet their time
to open like plums, *like sugar plums* —

it is not *yet* their time —

to cleave unto another
who is not *father-and-mother*

not their time to cleave, be cleft, break
in half, be halved, split
apart, joined

together again, becoming whole.

They *are* whole, *wholly* sensuous
indivisible, *perfect*
unto themselves, male and female, cleaving
to the sleeping seed within
(not knowing, even as they sleep,
the nation of desires *yet-to-be*).

THE CHILDREN
                    — the *AND* we are living for —
                                        ARE SLEEPING

IN DARKNESS

My plum, my sugar
plum, the Good Mother murmurs

as she looks at her child in sleep,
slipping down to the kitchen

to begin again
preparing the food for Christmas Day:

there are peaches, ripe and whole,
peaches waiting on the table

in a crystal bowl! The peaches are
steeping in brandy and cloves

          Did you hear a whisper this can't be so? —

I saw it with my very eyes:
the peaches were steeping in cloves, WHOLE *CLOVES*!

My peach, the Good Father murmurs
as he watches his child in sleep; he slips
downstairs, to prepare the wild dark berries
to have a smoke outside.   *My peach, my sugar*

68

plum, dumpling, plum
pudding, sweet

potato pie. When the children
of the Good Father close
their eyes, they close their eyes
unto themselves —
perfect,
   untouched, whole.

THE CHILDREN ARE SLEEPING IN DARKNESS

it is not yet their time

The Good Father
obeys the darkness, does not

disturb his children's sleep.
He does not eat his children's whole and perfect sleep!

THE CHILDREN ARE SLEEPING IN DARKNESS

   they are the WHOLE we're living for —

 THE GOOD FATHER DOES NOT EAT
 HIS CHILDREN'S SLEEP

 — Did you hear a whisper telling you this can't be so? —

I saw it the night of the solstice.
I saw it with my very eyes:

THE CHILDREN SLEEPING IN DARKNESS

They are   the plums

       sugar plums
               dancing

(in their sleep

          (   ) not a breath
                        of violation)

dancing in a forest — NO! — in a universe

     a cosmos,
          a galaxy,
               of   CLOVES!

EVERYTHING

    IS DANCING AND SHINING IN DARKNESS

    SWIMMING IN CLOVES —
                   WHOLE CLOVES!!!

— Did you hear a whisper — ?

IT DOESN'T MATTER WHAT YOU HEARD BEFORE

THE CHILDREN ARE SLEEPING

     (... you mean, simply falling asleep

     my eyes
        unopened, closed?   *)))*

   IT DOESN'T MATTER WHAT YOU HEARD BEFORE

The answers to — *the whispers —*

are as simple as   *violation* and its *lack*, the *WHOLENESS*
of its lack

The answers to   — *the whispers*   —

are as simple as a winter tale that   BELIEVES

THE CHILDREN ARE SLEEPING

The children are sleeping and
                    — *it is the AND we're living for* —

they sleep through the whole night and
then the darkness opens
            (((the darkness must love us   more than light
                    for it is the darkness that gives us
                    our visions and our light   )))
and the children open
their eyes, they open
the curtains; the stockings
will be opened as well as the presents and

                        EVERYTHING

IS MOVING
                EVERYTHING WILL HAPPEN FAST

            MUCH FASTER

than any other time of the year, this *fast* turning
to the light AND
                — *the AND we're living for* —

IT WILL BE *NOISY!*

Toys and nuts and trinkets and oranges scatter-spill
across the floor and the Good Mother
opens her big lap
and the Good Father opens juicy oranges —
with hands that smell of
tobacco, oatmeal and the fresh cold air outside —

and the arms

of the solstice tree will open to us
hold aloft
the halved and varnished walnut shells
which are holding
nests of flannel and *look* —

each one is holding

a tiny baby

each one is *untouched and WHOLE!*

— *this is the AND we're living for* —

IT DOESN'T MATTER
WHAT YOU'VE BEEN TOLD BEFORE

— this *AND* is the wholeness we are searching for —

(EVEN IN OUR LONGING
THAT DOES NOT RECOGNIZE ITSELF
AS *SEARCHING-FOR!)*

This is the season for opening.
This is the season for remaining closed.
This is the season we are becoming whole.

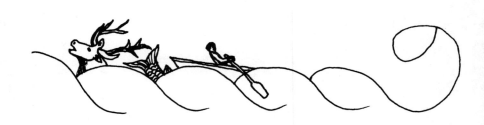

III
LULLABYE FOR
THE CHILD WITHIN

... AS IF GARDEN WERE OUR MOTHER TONGUE

> *Now that I'd launched myself into*
> *what I'd once ... considered "real life,"*
> *ordinary life was coming to seem exotic,*
> *like the trees I saw on the highway.*
>
> — Joyce Johnson

Something doesn't have to happen every day.

— Ntozake Shange

DEEP WINTER HAS TAKEN US OVER

We're so cold   our breath   looms
us larger than our frames
which have already grown up fat
and stout   leathered bulwarks
against the cold

we're so cold   our   rigid   shoulders
turn to the nose   for direction
but there's no spoor to sniff
in this alien cold

We're so cold   our mental state brittle
doesn't track   all the facts
our thick tongues   talk
scant: *de-ice   wind   skid   chill*

we're so cold   hard-pressed
for easy breathing   Our engine   chokes
its fat belly whines   for Cadbury bars
Art Song Chicken Wings To Go

> *It's cold here, real cold*
> *we're so cold, we're heavy with sleep*

We must numb our desires
harden into our shells
unlike our children   who dance their eager
voices out into the snow

where they lie down to rest
in the drifts   murmuring
we're so cold   where the frost
seeks permanence, branding
on every cheek a silver O

It's cold here, real cold
we're so cold, we're heavy with sleep

If only we weren't so exhausted, if only the exhaust
from the other machines
would make this engine sing
If only a Chinook
would blow us free and clear, the metal
impervious to cold

It's cold here, real cold
we're so cold, we're heavy with sleep

We must numb our desires, lift
our heavy machines, again, our mood, another
500 feet   We must cruise
over all of Greenland and dig
the sleepy children   out   with our bare cold hands

It's cold here, real cold
we're so cold, we're heavy with sleep

Our thick tongues tell us
it's all right   cleared for take-off
these wings heavy with sleep
my co-pilot   murmurs

Larry   we're falling   and yes
I know   we're falling to sleep
lifting and falling
over Greenland   to icy sleep

and we hit the ground
our legs   come back   free
of wool and steel and cold

we're not cold   we're running
off this glacier   we run
down to the green land
even faster than our dogs

down to the weeds and grasses
where we bury our faces
roll in the smell
of green   our bodies   breathe

deep   loosen   us   our warm
and softer   selves   our noses
grow thick   in the yellow
fuzz of camomile

and we exhale
the word

v e g e t a t i o n

as if we'll talk and run forever

as if we're young

as if *garden*

were our mother tongue

THREE VIEWS OF SUMMER

Morning, a woman's bare arm, crooked in the window. The curtains hardly flutter. Someone down the block is playing the piano. Arpeggios. Scales. Is she naked, does she sleep alone, are her toenails polished bronze? A Russian olive tree shivers silver in the heat.

Through the brush to the lake, close air and the tickle of thick-lipped blossoms. The smell of marsh hangs like sweat in wool. Why did we come here? Dozing insects. Cloud cover. A shimmer over the flat red rocks. Sunset breaks like oil across the water.

His half-shut eyes looked Asian, the open window black against the night. Fresh mint in the tea. He held the glass to my mouth. We took turns. I pulled the covers up to cool my shaking. He kissed my forehead. The curtains hardly fluttered.

#3

cuddling you
my hands encircle worlds   & my tongue
traces your

pale blue scar
the ancient seam that closed you male   where
my body

opens where
blue maps our longing for the ruby
embryo

which unfolds
itself at four weeks   a fat yolk sac
swelling limb-

buds   inner
pockets   nets of purple arteries
surrounding

one pulsing
undifferentiated phallus —
making love

we find this
primal union   (not yet divided
male   female   )

singing   the
single   bright   centering   magenta
sinew   we're

swimming o-
cean horses   engulfed by warm coral-
blue waters

we'll call our
cell walls permeable   feast on rich

placenta

SONG OF THE FISHERMAN'S LOVER

You stump your way through the tangled
brush, the rocky shore. Listen,
the light in the water
shimmies rainbows across my skin,
the amber sand, my belly
full of roe.

        I know the streams
freeze veins blue as ice,
rocks cut swifter than knives. The chill
you love so well turns gray, turns
glitter. Follow the smell. See
my speckles burn.

        I'll be glassy-eyed
and quick, teasing feathers, the silver
spinners. Nosing every inlet
I'll dance up over the hills and ridges
where waters rush deeper canyons
through white spray to thinner air.

Hurry. The last arch
to the highest waters. Wait madly
for this split suspension
in air. Then head and tail at once
the headfirst dive slaps
thousands of eggs
quivering down.

        Matted and drunk
with honey, you lumber from the brush.
Splash and growl. Say
slime and fur and waters draw
you into me. Dip me from the water.
Kiss the gash. Say *fish*.
Say *woman*.

MINNESOTA TROPICS

The elements have merged into solicitude.
— Louise Gluck

I   Meeting

In this thunder heat that turns inland
to tropics, the air hangs
thick and gold, street lights go turquoise
and the garden reaches
its ocean green — so alive
I feel Jim standing here by me.
It seems the orange crepe nasturtiums
refuse a proper mourning
floating as they do
airily above their lily pads, suspended
over webbing: creamy translucent cords.
I see the earth is ocean blue.
Call me soon, he said
remember   it's James L. White
in the phone book. I remember

he didn't laugh like a dying man.
Intent on everything around him, easily
laughing or serious, he opened himself
to our lives. And yet
I saw his life flash
before my eyes as if the four of us were all
already dead, watching the past,
the daily fuss, slip from us as smoothly
as the ripples an arm makes
languishing over the rim of a canoe.
I look at my garden, it is ocean blue.

We could have been strangers
seated together by chance
in the dining car, a train steaming
through Mexico, so calm this meeting,
freed from the usual hesitations.
After midnight in that first cool black
that lets your breath
not shirk the flowered air, I mentioned
my habit, waiting up for the easy
breathing time, *I finally feel*
like myself. When he said
What a wonderful line, I offered
it to him. *No, I don't want to take*
anyone's lines anymore —
and I'm not revising. Do you
think that's all right?

And, yes, all right, is that enough to tell —
other than how we said good-bye?
Jim said it, Like Old Married People,
years of habit, which car, which
side. Unlikely quartet, merged
into solicitude. In parting we saw
the separate public selves: Sand and
Khaki, Flowers and Jeans, Gypsy Glitter,
Earthy Chenille. Unlikely quartet —
old friends, just met, not knowing
if right now for the first time
or long ago
or any minute again
we will slip the flan into our mouths
from each other's spoons.

II Lullabye

Good-bye friends more full of life than lovers
    trading outrageous stories many hours of the night
        in this very restaurant where a lover left me
            his shirt moving in and out
                of the purple garden behind him on the wall

Good-bye restaurant   good-bye talk
    who-drinks-too-much   what-not-to-tell
        Good-bye fantasies talked out loud
            islands   Ireland   Egypt   camels without filters
                Good-bye what-you'd-like-I'll-bring-next-time
                    purple cosmos from my garden   *The Wishing Bone*:
                        a book

Good-bye books in the bookstore light
    where our hands took up each and every book
        Did you read it   did you love it?
            Good-bye each book
                Body Rags & its loveliest cover of any book
            Good-bye words in poems   *salt   photograph   bones*
                Good-bye last   call
                    laughing words last of all   *Don't wait   drive on*

Good-bye First Avenue   jazz   around the corner
    not too far to town
        fences weaving the streetlight's lace
            Good-bye   memory   *empanada*   Santa Fe   adobe
                cool against my palm
                    the sudden   luscious   smell of sage
                        Good-bye pillow   next to hands

Good-bye Mother   Father   &   your mysterious room
    the hills and valleys of your chenille bedspread
        Good-bye lovers every one

Good-bye miracle godchild
        the surprising way
            you gripped my chest
        Good-bye fingers   thumb
            touching   holding   wanting more

        good-bye   this lust
                    to save you

III Sweathouse

In the mourning heat, the garden lies
too bright to see. Moss roses open their
papery selves, corn silks dazzle
purple in the shimmer, green growth wavers
in the light. Sweat-throbbing salt
and Santa Fe. This air   is   sticky
aloe vera, I feel weak, sweat
like anger wells up in the heat.
Maybe that line about the night
was weak, but Jim gave it back, it's
what I've got. Mad and rushed
I chop up scraps, limes
and eggshells, skins of alligator
pears, they froth over the garden
like ocean foam. This loving, giving
taking away. Too much for me to see.

IV Dream

From the center of the garden
where the purple cosmos tilt and float
Brigitte waves
a giant   leaf, it's lavender,
woven pale and lacy-cool
and from its tip
a reaching vine curls
intently up to air. Tassles
trail back and brush my hands
and the fan itself
which I see now is a living
heart. It cools me, breathes:

Slow down. Let the garden grow
thick and lush. In your hands
the aloe vera thrives. Give up
self-loathing. Give up revising.
Give up the rush of grief. Say
you'll be yourself in this day's heat
in night air, be easy breathing
anywhere. The garden grows
thick and lush. Honor
the living life. Give in
to loving. Give in, your life.

LETTER TO JOAN

Dear Joan, when you and I were first friends, saving the ghetto in miniskirts, the issue of names seemed trivial. But now I'm writing to ask, please stop calling me *Rose*. My mother, groggy in the hospital after twilight sleep, thought of her dear friend Rose and signed the birth certificate two words: *Rose Ann*. Everybody said it one word: *Roseann*. Where I grew up, everybody had double fancy names: Alice Jane, Jane Ann, Anna De Genira. It was, in fact, this very Anna De Genira, my gramma, who made up a nickname I really liked, because it was funny, *Rosie*, the happy kid who made her laugh out loud, the one who mugged for the camera, danced on the cellar door. But both these names got lost in the formal North where computers go by legal and spell out identities *married-first-maiden-middle*, no room for my middle — technology baptized me the single, solitary *Rose*.

It haunted me, played into my fears, the ancient romance of the Rose. Frail beauty. Intense blossoming on the brink of destruction. The elegance. The glamorous suffering. The unspeakable doom. And the romance of the men who murmur *Darling Rose, Rose of Sharon, My Rose*. My brothers drawl the slow Ozark way, *Here's to the Rose*, and feed the jukebox *Second-hand, Wild Irish, Rambling, San Antonio . . .*

I'm giving up my flirtation with this tragic identity, good-hearted woman who comes to no good end. I'm giving up the woman of mystery, Faye Dunaway in Chinatown, and the dark rose glow of booze. *China doll, alcohol.* I'm living in a more ordinary way. I need a name that's plain.

You say that I'm the one careful to remember, to hyphenate your *maiden-married*. Will you be the one to forget? My old name stuffed to the back of the stocking drawer, a dusty rose petal sachet. Anna De Genira named a happy child. And that name brings both of them back. Grandmother, child. Learning how to ask, I am, faithfully, your chum, with love, as ever, Rosie

10 ONE-LINERS FOR 1984

1. 1984 is the year I laughed outloud, driving
   in my car, the moment
   I realized George Orwell didn't tell me
   I'd turn 40 in 1984

2. 1984 is the year I drove all over the freeways
   happy to get on the L.A. freeway, crazy
   for the roads through Northern Minnesota
   where a motel has a swimming pool in the shape of Minnesota
   and a restaurant that serves
   TORSK ALFREDO & TORSK ALMONDINE

3. 1984 is the year I visualized my women friends driving
   all over this country
   when I learned Jack Kerouac never learned to drive a car

4. 1984 is the year I marked the passing
   of many who led me through my childhood:

   Indira Gandhi, Richard Brautigan, Marvin Gaye,
   Anna De Genira Lloyd

5. 1984 is the year lots of us feel old, shocked to see kids
   carrying signs for Reagan, all their mamas did
   raise their babies up to be cowboys
   voting for the cowboy who lies

6. 1984 is the year America looks like a rhinestone cowboy
   glitter mirrors on the buildings
   white freeways over poverty
   sparkling jewelry on TV

7. 1984 is the year Big Brother doesn't have to watch
   anyone on TV
   because everybody's too busy for revolution
   watching *The Prisoner* and MTV

8. 1984 is the year the people of Poland
   hauled a car to the graveyard
   lifted open the trunk
   and made a chrêche of Christmas tree lights and a baby doll
   for the murdered priest, solidarity

9. 1984 is the year we were lucky
   to hear Geraldine Ferraro in our own lifetime
   & lucky again to hear at last
   why Freud betrayed us —
   the books of Janet Malcolm, Jeff Masson, & Alice Miller
   carry us along

10. 1984 is the year there's no Prince of Peace
    there's just Prince, crawling through his basement window
    there's Geraldine, undaunted Queen of Hearts
    there's Doris Lessing, jiving *The New York Times*
    there's Tina Turner, pouring out energy for all of us over 40
    and there's Bruce Springsteen on the road
    telling the Right Wing he's not singing for them

    and I'm riding in my car, turning on the radio
    American as any cowboy mama
    I'm driving fine, feeling free,
    driving in the U.S.A.

AUGUST

poem in which DARK is a friendly word

Way past bedtime   branches rear up
whinny against the window screen
GHOST IN THE GRAVEYARD   the children
scream   accost each other
in the dark   their voices
hoarse   at once   and shrill   I feel   the
thudding of their running
sunk back in my smoky couch
with its shiny foliage and darkening pastels
I am reading the words   *rose   chenille*
I am thinking the words   *my   daughter*
is   in   her   childhood   and I am falling
into that thrilling cricket-dark
my gramma's open window   the tatting
on the dusky chair
It all comes back easy
like the fall to dying   in summer's
harvest-heavy air   Sometimes it seems
too long a wait   to follow my childhood
there   I want August   with me here
forever   I want children   running
strong   and   hoarse — the sweet
dark   heat

THE GROSS POEM:
CONFESSIONS OF THE TEN-YEAR-OLD

Oh, gross! Mushy tofu, slimy
seeds, tomato guts, a rabbit
skinned and put in a pot.
There's fur in that water, don't
let it touch me, Mom, it's gross.

Hair in the bathtub, hairs
on my toothbrush, hair
in my mother's armpit — all the old ones
are hairy and gross.
Big legs, big butts, big boobs.
Don't sit in their lap, you'll
get smothered to death by their bad
breath. They stink because
they drink wine, eat shrimps,
smoke nasty cigarettes.

And that's not the worst of it:
the old ones kill animals,
they don't even *care*. They laugh
about boogers, say the F--- word,
smooch each other on their mouths
and at night
they snore and groan.

Babies
are just as bad. Whatever you do
don't look at them when they eat.
Their food runs back
out of their mouth. They will smear
wet crackers on your shirt.
They are gross. I'm glad
I'm not one of them
anymore — I suppose the reason
my mom could stand to take care of me is
because she
is so fat and gross.

I'm happy just the way I am now.
I comb my hair just right — feathered —
tuck my turtleneck tight
inside my jeans. I eat apples,
alfalfa sprouts, cheese
in separate plasti-wrap, bread
that's slim reminds me
how I'm skinny, my muscles
strong as any boy. I can make
perfect angels in the snow.
At night, coyote and me run the woods,
call out to the moon, *Never
grow old,
never grow old.*

THE BEST ELEGY
IS THE ONE THAT CONJURES THE SPIRIT

Philip, come back, it's Halloween —
there's a black star on my cheek
but I can't remember how
to make up scary faces on my kids.
Was it three blue lines under the eyes?
A red slash down the lip
to the chin? Lurking
in wigs and taffeta capes, we
played the monster better than anyone.

But you, brother, took the childhood games
to heart. Now young boys
with tight-drawn cheeks mill
through a giant hall. From the stage, the amps
echo and squeal. You strut
and sputter, Lon Chaney
on keyboards, his whiteface
wails, *They elected me monster* and the boys
lift you up on their shoulders, they
bring sweets and pillows,
pills and women, wine and furs.

Lastborn, anybody's monkey
hunched on your back, tonight you
should be here with us, homeless
as ever. You pick up
the fattest pumpkin, draw
your knife full-circle, free-hand through
the crusted shell. Clean
out the stringy flesh. You
carve and mutter to the kids *Nightmares
are only pretend:*

Pointed ears for Jack
Split teeth for Jill
Dimples for the boy who can't sit still
A wink for the girl who flashed out of reach
And slits for the lessons nobody can teach.

Lights off,
you pour the brandy,
stick the seeds in the oven to roast.
Oh, Jack-O-Lanterns!
Your grim candles make grim faces,
shadow-monsters going up
in smoke. The fire play
draws us in again, arm-in-arm
with all our hearts. Toothless, we grin
inside this bright and breathing cave
where you sit cross-legged
before the balanced and shifting
sticks of the fire.

EAVESDROPPING FROM THE OTHER ROOM, I HEAR MY BROTHER'S DAUGHTER TELL MY DAUGHTER THE FACTS OF LIFE

When you get born, Anna
the first father is your legal father
unless you get adopted
so you don't have to worry the way I do
because you're already adopted
and your mom's your legal mother and your real mother
and that woman you were born from —
she's your body-mother.

I already know that, Lisa. You know
I call Rosie my real mom
and that other one —
I call her *my old home.*
Before I came here
I lived in her, I had to live
somewhere. Did you think I came from the sun?

Eavesdropping from the other room
I want to say *yes*   and   hug them both
but I don't. They already know
we played *Here Comes the Sun*   over and over
when they were born. Little darling,
littlest pigtail. Already half-grown
on ABBEY ROAD, Nina Simone. They already know
the day John Lennon got shot
I cried out NO in bed, cried out
for the child he lost, is losing now this way:
the child taken from him by flashes
of fire, pieces of lead.

Praise the morning radiance!
The days we lived to see our children live,
wherever they came from —
old   sun   home — already
giving birth to their own separate lives,
already being borne away.

TRIBE

i lost my baby
            it slipped away
    quick as a fish
                    dances
        out of your hands
    i lost my baby
                the other children say
        we want
                    to see it   bury it
    it was so small
                    i say   but my hands
            too want to dig
                        they took
            to writing
                    but the slips kept
            slipping away
    the children persist   say   *what*
            did they do with it then?
        throw it
                    in the river?
            throw it away?
    it was so small
                    i say   evasive
        as a fish
                    i see its shape
        slipping across   the
                        doctor's tv screen
        ghost sac: they called it
            couldn't tell me why
            it went
    away   why
                we can't bury it
            here
                    on the alluvial plain
    downstream
                    another lost baby
            found

99

by an anthropologist who
    says the burial
    6,000 years ago
was performed
with dignity
the baby
        curled up
like it's still inside
    its mother
the baby
    buried
    with ceremony even though
        it died at birth
    because
            of a spine
    that didn't close
                the doctors
    can't tell me what part
of my baby
        didn't open, close:
fingers, spine, lungs, nose

how much   how little   there is
    to know   i see
        the baby's mother bending
    over
      the grave
                my hands want
    her hands' motion:
                dig   wrap   hold

denied a grave
            my hands
    dig anyway
                slip in the hole   sand
and peat and a young birch tree
    it is so small i say
                yet the leaves
    already dance silver   in the wind

like a fish in the river
ghosts of all the children
lost to us
                    in or out of graves
children dancing
along this river
the river that dances
down
            the alluvial plain

POEM FOR MY SISTER, ON THE OCCASION OF HER WITHDRAWAL FROM NICOTINE

after "The Sisters of Sexual Treasure," by Sharon Olds

When my sister and I
left the joyless house of childhood
all we wanted
was the pursuit of joy —
all drugs were choice
especially the cigarette, yes, the cigarette
in the mouth.

But now in our middle years
as we try to find some middle ground
between excess and deprivation
try to get grounded instead of high,
muttering with W. C. Fields,
"It's easy to quit, I've done it
a thousand times,"

we look at our daughters
and wonder
what kind of childhood
they carry with them. After all,
we have no idea what it's like
to have mothers who play the Rolling Stones
for Christmas — Dionysus over
Jesus any day.

When THE BIG CHILL is over, my sister's daughter
turns to her and says:

    Mom, when that woman played
    the organ at the funeral
    why did they leave out
    the part with the angels?

The angels, my sister says, what angels?

> You know, Mom, on that record
> you always play
> in the beginning
> there's a whole lot of angels
> and they're singing way up high:
> *you can't always get what you want*
> *but if you try*
> *you may find*
> *that sometimes   you get what you need.*

Sister, when I look at our daughters
who are finding their own angels
and when I look at you
without that cigarette in your hand
the cigarette
you want so bad

I feel a rush of gratitude and say   again
with Ntozake Shange:

> *i found god within myself/*
> *& i loved her/ i loved her fiercely*

WHAT IS IT LIKE TO BE INDIRA GANDHI?

What would it be like to be Indira Gandhi?
Do you mean
what would it be like for me
to be Indira Gandhi?
If I am being her, where does she go?
What would happen to the vacuum in my body?
Or do we trade places? Would two souls collapse
into one? And go back and forth?
No, no, what I mean is
what is it like for Indira Gandhi to be Indira Gandhi?
You might as well ask what is it like
to speak in Hindi? To walk barefoot in the garden?
What is it like to be Indira Gandhi
for the millions of native Hindi speakers
who have no idea what it is like to be a head of state —
much less what it is like for Indira Gandhi to be Indira Gandhi. . . .
What is it like to be a head of state?
What is it like to rest in state,
to hear the crowds shouting "immortal, immortal"?
What is it like to lie on a bed of sandalwood
dressed in a robe of flowers?
What is it like to watch
your son touch your third eye with fire?
What is it like
to watch your soul rise with the smoke,
your bones scattered
across 13 sacred rivers?
What is it like to be Indira Gandhi?

What is it like to be Indira Gandhi?

SAY HELLO

saying hello
was much harder than running a marathon
harder than getting up and starting the car
at 30 below
saying hello
reminds you   you didn't want to
you wanted to stay in your bolt-hole
saying hello
is a tribute to the hope you hoped was there
no matter how much is taken away
there's always something left
saying hello
is good-bye to mornings on the couch
giving up the loss you wanted to hoard
I want to say *I'm not that dumb*
it's just that I was awfully shy
I want to say *there's nothing smarter*
than saying hello
hello echoes through your body
the way your voice echoed through the drainage pipes
along the ditch   you knew
the flash floods wouldn't sweep you away
you knew you could make it to the other side   calling out
hello   hello
is the echo of hope for yourself
for the particular days of childhood
you had no reason to suppress
the glider swing in the back yard
the morning you woke up excited to run through the grass
and when you got to the garden
you announced the first sentence of your life
I see Gramma
saying hello
is the soles of the new feet
pressed firmly into the inky pad
ignorant of all the good-byes to come
don't say good-bye

good-bye comes soon enough
whether or not you've been saying hello
say hello

say hello

for Deborah and Stephen and the birth of Baby Joe

Photo by Allen Simpson

ABOUT THE AUTHOR

Roseann Lloyd lives in Minneapolis with her family. *Tap Dancing for Big Mom* is her first collection of poetry. She has also published essays, cartoons, and prose meditations. Her current project is translating a Norwegian novel by Herbjørg Wassmo, which will be published next year by Seal Press.